R

Learn Ruby In 24 Hours Or Less

A Beginner's Guide to Learning Ruby Programming Now

Table Of Contents

Introduction

In this book you will find the fundamental aspects of the Ruby programming language. It will explain theories and lessons through detailed instructions and practical examples. With this eBook, you'll learn how to get Ruby, how to write Ruby statements, and how to use this language in creating your own programs.

If you're searching for a comprehensive learning material for Ruby, this is the book you need. With the help of the important ideas and practical examples contained within, you will be able to master Ruby quickly even if you have never programmed anything before. By reading this material, you will become an effective Ruby programmer in 24 hours (or even less).

Here are some of the things you'll learn from this eBook:

- How to download the right version of Ruby for your computer

- The fundamental principles of Ruby programming

- The methods that you can use in Ruby

- How to handle program exceptions

- The syntax of Ruby commands

- How to create loops, iterators, classes, objects, variables, and many more

Let's begin the journey.

Chapter 1: How to Get Started

This eBook will teach you how to use the Ruby programming language. It will provide you with codes, explanations, and practical examples. Before discussing how Ruby works, however, you need to install this language first.

In this chapter, you will learn how to get, install, and launch Ruby.

The Terminal

Software manufacturers have released several IDEs (i.e. Integrated Development Environment) for the Ruby language. However, you will surely spend some time using your computer's terminal (also known as the "shell prompt" or "command prompt"). The "terminal" is the small window that accepts and runs commands. If your machine runs on Windows or Linux, it's likely that you have used a terminal before.

To launch the terminal on a Windows-based computer, click on the Start button and hit "Run." Then, type "cmd.exe" in the dialogue box. For Linux computers, look for a program named "Terminal" or go to the "Applications" directory. Next, click on "Accessories" and launch the "Terminal" program. If your machine is a Mac, click on "Applications" and "Utilities." Then, look for the program named "Terminal.app."

You'll know that you succeeded if your screen displays a new window. This window should have a prompt and a banner. To make sure that you are looking at the right window, type "echo sample" and hit the Enter key. The window should display "sample".

How to Install Ruby

It's possible that you don't have to download Ruby anymore. Mac and Linux computers have preinstalled versions of the Ruby language. You can check whether your computer has Ruby by typing "ruby -v".

Installation is required for computers that don't have Ruby or those that have old versions of the language. Well, you don't have to worry since the installation process is easy and simple. You can install Ruby in two ways: (1) by downloading a pre-built distribution, or (2) by building it yourself. To keep this book simple, let's focus on the first method: getting a pre-built "distro" for your machine.

The Installation Process

Pre-built distributions are the best option for inexperienced programmers. With this kind of distribution, you won't have to code or compile anything. You'll just download the package and run it on your computer. Each OS (i.e. operating system) requires its own pre-built distribution. That means you can't run a Linux package on a Windows computer.

The drawback of installing a pre-built distro is that it doesn't allow any form of customization. If you're okay with this drawback, go ahead and download the right Ruby package for your computer.

Here are the steps you need to take when installing a pre-built package:

For Windows Computers:

Ruby packages come with a wide range of "gems" and libraries. Programmers refer to these packages as OCI (i.e. One-Click Installer). To get the latest built-in packages, visit this site: http://rubyforge.org/projects/rubyinstaller.

For Linux Computers:

Almost all Linux systems (e.g. Ubuntu) use "apt-get" to locate and install programs. You can install Ruby on your Linux computer by logging in as root, launching a terminal, and typing the following code:

apt-get install ruby2.3 libruby2.3 libreadline-ruby2.3 irb2.3

apt-get install rdoc2.3 ri2.3

The code given above will install Ruby 2.3 on your computer. This is the latest version of the language as of the time of writing.

Important Note: The code given above won't work if you don't have "root access" on your computer.

For Macintosh Computers:

Mac computers have built-in versions of Ruby. However, most of these versions are dated. If you want to get the latest versions, you need to visit www.macports.org and download the "MacPorts" program. Then, log in as root and type:

port install ruby23

This command will install Ruby 2.3 on your Mac. Alternatively, you may visit http://rubyosx.com and find the right package for your OS.

How to Run the Language

After installing Ruby, you surely want to launch some applications. Ruby is unique in that you can run it in two ways: (1) type codes interactively, or (2) create and run files. The former is an excellent way to get familiarized with the Ruby language. The latter is ideal for complex and/or redundant codes.

Let's discuss these methods in detail:

Typing Codes Interactively

Often, Ruby programmers use Ruby by entering it on a terminal. The example given below contains two important parts: "puts" and "^D". In this code, "puts" is an expression while "^D" is a character that ends the Ruby file.

% ruby

puts "This is a test."

^D

This is a test.

Important Note: This is one of the simplest techniques available. However, it makes typo errors extremely frustrating.

Most users utilize a tool called "irb" (i.e. Interactive Ruby) to run Ruby in an interactive manner. Basically, Interactive Ruby is a tool that has job control and line-editing capabilities. It also remembers the commands you have previously entered.

To launch this tool, you just have to type "irb" on a terminal. After this, you may enter your Ruby codes. The tool will evaluate your Ruby codes as you type them. That means you'll know whether you are entering the right codes or not. To close this tool, you may type "exit" or press your computer's end-of-file character (i.e. either CTRL + Z or CTRL + D).

The examples given below will show you two Ruby expressions and how they will appear in irb:

% irb

sum(5, 6)

=> 11

sum("butter", "fly")

=> "butterfly"

exit

Ruby Applications

Most Ruby programmers write applications using multiple files. They use an IDE (e.g. NetBeans) or text editor (e.g. vim, Notepad, Emacs, etc.) to generate and manage these files. You may run existing files in three ways: (1) using your IDE, (2) using your text editor, or (3) using your system's terminal. If you are dealing with a single-file program, you should use your preferred text editor. For complex programs or those that involve different files, you should use either a terminal or an IDE.

At this point, let's create a basic program and execute it. Launch a terminal. Then, create a new directory using the following commands:

mkdir \RubyProjects (for Windows)

mkdir RubyProjects (for Linux)

mkdir ~/RubyProjects (for Unix)

Next, access the new directory using one of these commands:

cd \RubyProjects (for Windows)

cd RubyProjects (for Linux)

cd ~/RubyProjects (for Unix)

Once you are inside the RubyProjects directory, access your favorite text editor and type the following expressions:

puts "It has been a great day."

puts "Unfortunately, it's already #{Time.now}"

Then, save the file and name it "program.rb".

You may launch a Ruby application using its filename. Launch your Ruby interpreter and enter the name of the program you want to run. For example, you can access the program.rb program just by typing its filename on your interpreter. The last two lines of the code below shows the output of the program:

$ ruby program.rb

It has been a great day.

Unfortunately, it's already 2016-4-23 09:03:46

Chapter 2: The Basics of the Ruby Language

This chapter will teach you the fundamental elements of Ruby. Read this material carefully – it contains information that will serve as the basis for other chapters.

Object-Oriented Programming

Ruby is considered as an object-oriented computer language, just like C#, PHP5 and Python. The changes that you'll make are applied on objects. Additionally, those changes result to new objects.

While writing an object-oriented program, you'll usually use model ideas from the physical world. You'll use codes to represent the things you're dealing with. In the Ruby language, you'll represent these things by defining classes. Each class contains a state and one or more methods that can work on that state.

Usually, you need to create an instance for each class. It's important to point out that "object" and "class instance" are considered as synonyms. In Ruby, you should use a constructor (i.e. a method linked to a class) to create an object. This language uses "new" as its default constructor. Analyze the example given below:

music1 = Music.new("Hotel California")

music2 = Music.new("Sweet Child of Mine")

Both of these instances came from a class named "Music." However, each instance has distinct properties. For example, each object has an identifier (also called "object ID"). Additionally, each object can hold one or more instance variables (i.e. variables that contain data unique to the instance that holds them). An instance variable holds the "state" of an object. In the example above, each song has a unique variable that stores the title of the song.

You may specify instance methods inside each class. Methods are sets of functionalities that you may invoke in the class' context. In turn, these methods can access the state and instance variables of an object. For example, the "Music" class may have a method named "play." If a variable points to an object, you may invoke the "play" method of that object and listen to a song.

You can invoke methods by sending messages to objects. These messages contain the name of the method, as well as the parameters it needs. After receiving a message, an object will check its class and search for the right method. If successful, the method will run.

These messages and methods might sound complex. However, they are extremely simple in practice. It's time to analyze some method invocations. For this example, you'll use "puts" (i.e. a method that prints its argument) and add a newline character before the next expression:

puts "Sample".index("a")

puts "test box.".length

puts sam.play(music)

That code produces:

2

3

boom, boom, boom ...

These lines show methods being invoked as arguments for "puts."
Each argument has two parts, the "receiver" (i.e. the word at the
left-hand side of the dot) and the method (i.e. the word after the
dot).

Basic Stuff

Syntax rules can be extremely boring, particularly for inexperienced programmers. Because of that, you'll learn about syntax rules later. This part of the book will focus on the things you'll use to create Ruby applications.

For now, let's create a basic Ruby application. The method that you'll use here prints a greeting on the terminal. In this example, let's call that method several times:

```ruby
def say_hi(user_name)

  result = "Hi, " + user_name

  return result

end


# Personalized greeting

puts say_hi("Mark")

puts say_hi("Mary")
```

As you can see, the syntax of Ruby is clean and simple. You won't have to terminate statements using semicolons if you'll write these statements on different lines. To add a comment, you'll just use the "#" symbol. Additionally, this language isn't strict when it comes to code layout. Your programs won't produce errors even if you won't place any indentation in your code. However, indentations are recommended since they ensure code readability.

You need to use the "def" keyword to define a method. After this keyword, you need to specify the method's identifier as well as its parameters. You may enclose the parameters using parentheses to make your code readable. This language doesn't require curly braces when delimiting compound definitions and statements. Rather, you just have to use the "end" keyword to terminate your definitions or statements.

In this example, you defined a method and called it twice. In each of these cases, you forwarded the output to the "puts" method. Keep in mind that "puts" simply prints its argument on the terminal and adds a newline character (i.e. the character you'll get after hitting the Enter key). Here's the output that you'll get after running the code given above:

Hi, Mark

Hi, Mary

The expression *"puts say_hi("Mark")"* has two method invocations. The first one calls the "say_hi" method while the second one calls the "puts" method.

In addition, the current example involves some string objects. The Ruby programming language offers different ways to generate string objects. The most popular approach, however, involves the utilization of string literals. Basically, a string literal is a sequence of characters placed between quotation marks (i.e. single quotes or double quotes).

There's a difference between using single quotes and double quotes in your codes. In general, Ruby doesn't alter the characters you'll place between single quotation marks. Thus, the value of the string is identical to the characters you typed. Double quotes, on the other hand, require Ruby to do some work. With double quotation marks, Ruby needs to search for substitutions (i.e. character sequences that begin with "\") and replace them with the right binary values. The most common substitution is "\n", which adds a new line to the code. Newline characters become line breaks if the string that contains them is an output. Here's an example:

puts "This sample \nis awesome."

output:

This sample

is awesome.

As mentioned earlier, Ruby replaces strings with binary values. Programmers refer to this functionality as "expression interpolation." Basically, Ruby replaces "#{expression} with the expression's value. You can use this functionality to rewrite the "say_hi" method:

```ruby
def say_hi(user_name)
  result = "Hi, #{user_name)"
  return result
end
puts say_hi('Mark')
```

output:

Hi, Mark

Ruby will search for the value of "user_name" during the creation of the object. Then, it will pass the value to the new object. This language allows you to place complex expressions in your #(expression) construct. For the example given below, you will call a method called "capitalize" to print the parameter and make sure that the initial letter is in uppercase:

```ruby
def say_hi(user_name)
  result = "Hi, #{user_name.capitalize}"
  return result
end
puts say_hi('Mark')
```

output:

Hi, Mark

Important Note: You'll learn about strings and other data types later.

Lastly, you may further simplify the "say_hi" method. Keep in mind that Ruby methods don't return the value of all expressions they evaluate. Only the value of the most recent expression will be returned. That means you can eliminate the return clause and temporary variable. Here's the code:

def say_hi(user_name)

  "Hi, #{user_name.capitalize}"

end

puts say_hi('Mark')

output:

Hi, Mark

The Naming Convention of Ruby

The Ruby language uses a unique convention for naming objects. Basically, it uses the first character of an identifier to determine the purpose of that identifier. You should use an underscore or a lowercase letter to start the name of a method, a parameter, or a local variable. You should type "$" before the name of a global variable. The identifier of an instance variable, on the other hand, should start with "@".

You should add "@@" before the name of a class variable. Lastly, you should use an uppercase letter when naming a constant, a module, or a class. The table given below will help you understand Ruby's naming convention:

Local	Class	Global	Instance	Class and Constant
sample	@@auto mobile	$design	@laptop	Bowling
_99	@@aircr aft	$plan	@compu ter	Fruit
e_theory	@@food	$trick	@door	Gadget
bar_b_q	@@hobb y	$tips	@stone	Tree

After the first character, you may combine numbers, letters, and underscores to create a unique name. However, you can't place a number right after the "@" symbol. You need to divide multiword variables by placing an underscore between each word pair. Additionally, you need to capitalize the first letter of each word. The name of a method may end with "=", "!", or "?".

Hashes and Arrays

The hashes and arrays of the Ruby language are collections of objects. Both contain sets of objects that you can asses through a "key." Hashes allow you to use any type of object as your key. Arrays, on the other hand, require you to use integers as keys. Both hashes and arrays expand to contain more elements. Arrays offer excellent efficiency when it comes to accessing objects. However, hashes provide great flexibility. Hashes and arrays may contain objects from different data types. Thus, you may create a hash to store a string and an integer.

You should use array literals (i.e. sets of elements written between brackets) to generate an array object. Once you have an array, you may access its elements by entering an index between a pair of square brackets. As the next example shows, the indices of Ruby start from zero.

x = [5, 'alligator', 9.99]   *# basic array that contains three elements*

puts = "The third element of the array is #{x[2]}"

 # modify the first element

x[0] = 6

puts "The elements of the array are #{x.inspect}"

output:

The third element of the array is 9.99

The elements of the array are [6, "alligator", 9.99]

The current example involves a special value called "nil." In most computer languages, the term nil refers to the absence of any object. In the Ruby language, however, nil has a different meaning: it is an object that doesn't represent anything.

Creating word-based arrays can be difficult, particularly because of the commas and quotation marks. Fortunately, the Ruby language offers a shortcut: "%w". Analyze the example below:

x = ['knight', 'bishop', 'king', 'queen', 'pawn']

x[2]   #   "king"

x[4]   #   "pawn"

 # the code given below produces the same result:

x = %w{ knight bishop king queen pawn }

x[2]   #   "king"

x[4]   #   "pawn"

A hash is similar to an array. Hash literals require curly braces instead of square brackets. Its literals should provide two objects per item: the value and the key. You must separate these objects using "=>".

For instance, you can map songs to the artists who sang them. The hash given below will show you how:

```
songs_artists = {

'If You Could See Me Now' => 'The Script'

'Night Changes'    => 'One Direction'

'Love Yourself'    => 'Justin Bieber'


}
```

The words on the left-hand side of the code serve as the keys. The ones on the right-hand side, meanwhile, are the values. In Ruby, each key should be unique – you'll get an error if you'll enter 'Love Yourself' twice.

Similar to arrays, you need to use square brackets to index hashes. For the current example, you should use a method called "p" to print values on a terminal. This method is similar to "puts." The only difference is that "p" prints values explicitly.

```
p songs_artists[ 'Night Changes' ]

p songs_artists[ 'If You Could See Me Now' ]

p songs_artists[ 'Love Yourself' ]

p songs_artists[ 'Like a Virgin' ]
```

output:

"One Direction"

"The Script"

"Justin Bieber"

nil

As you can see, hashes return "nil" whenever you enter an invalid index. This is a convenient feature most of the time, since "nil" is equivalent to "false" if used in a conditional expression. However, Ruby lets you change this feature. For instance, if you want to know how many times each particular word occurs within a file, you may set zero (i.e. "0") as your default value. Here, you can set words as keys and just increase the corresponding value.

Symbols

While programming, you usually need to set the name of each significant object. For instance, you may set a name for each compass point. Here's an example:

EAST   = 1

WEST   = 2

NORTH = 3

SOUTH = 4

You may use these names for the remaining part of your code.

Here's an example:

walk(SOUTH)

look(WEST)

Important Note: In most cases, the numeric value of a constant is not important (it just needs to be unique).

The Ruby language offers a simpler alternative. A symbol is a constant name that doesn't require pre-declaration. Additionally, a symbol is unique 100% of the time. Symbol literals begin with ":". Check the examples below:

walk(:SOUTH)

look(:WEST)

You don't have to set any value for your symbols—Ruby will do that on your behalf. Additionally, Ruby makes sure that a symbol will retain its value regardless of its position in the application. The code below will illustrate this idea:

def walk(compass_point)

  if compass_point == :SOUTH

  # ...

  end

end

Ruby programmers often use symbols in hashes. You may use symbols to rewrite the "songs_artists" example given above:

```
songs_artists {
  :If You Could See Me Now      =>   ' The Script ',
  :Night Changes       =>   ' One Direction ',
  :Love Yourself       =>   ' Justin Bieber '
}
songs_artists[:Love Yourself]    # →   "Justin Bieber"
songs_artists[:Night Changes]    # →   "One Direction"
```

The Control Structures

Ruby supports all of the popular control structures (e.g. while loops, if statements, etc.). C, Perl, and Java programmers might be confused since Ruby doesn't require braces to enclose statements. Rather, this language uses the "end" keyword to terminate code blocks. Here's an example:

```
if timer > 5
  puts "You won"
elseif tries == 0
  puts "You lost"
else
  puts "Please enter any number"
  end
```

Important Note: You may also use "end" to terminate a "while" statement.

Almost all Ruby statements produce a value. Thus, you can use these statements as conditions. The method called "gets," for instance, prints "nil" if it reaches the end of the program or the succeeding line of the input stream. Since Ruby considers "nil" as "false" when used in a conditional statement, you may type the following:

while sample = gets

  puts sample.downcase

end

This code assigns the "line" variable to nil or the next portion of the text. Then, "while" will evaluate the resulting value. The loop will stop if the value is nil.

You can use a statement modifier as a shortcut if your conditional statement involves one expression only. You just have to type the expression, enter "while" or "if", then specify your condition. Here's a basic example:

if temperature > 100

  puts "It is extremely hot"

end

Let's rewrite that code using a modifier:

puts "It is extremely hot" if temperature > 100

Important Note: Perl users are surely familiar with statement modifiers.

The Regular Expressions

The built-in data types (e.g. arrays, strings, integers, etc.) of Ruby are similar to that of other computer languages. However, only scripting languages (e.g. awk, Perl, Ruby, etc.) support regular expressions. This is unfortunate since regular expressions can be powerful when you are working on text-based data.

Basically, you can use regular expressions to specify character patterns that must be matched. As a Ruby programmer, you will create this kind of expression by enclosing a pattern using two slash characters. Additionally, since you are using Ruby, a regular expression is an object so you can manipulate it as such.

The expression given below creates a basic pattern. This pattern compares one pattern against one or more text strings:

/Book|Magazine/

As you can see, you must delimit a pattern using two forward slashes. The pattern contains two strings that you are trying to match. A "|" symbol separates these strings. The pipe symbol requires the system to choose either the left-hand string or the right-hand one.

Code Blocks

A "code block" is a piece of code that you can link to method calls. Because of this, code blocks have a lot of similarities with typical parameters. Programmers consider this as one of Ruby's most powerful features.

You may use a code block to execute callbacks, to pass pieces of code around, and to execute iterators.

A code block is a group of statements written between "do... end" or between a pair of curly braces. Here's an example:

{ puts "This code is awesome" }

Here's another one:

do

  music.play(song)

  song.listen

end

You will associate code blocks with method calls 100% of the time. You can achieve this by inserting the block into the line that holds the method invocation. The code below will illustrate this idea:

say { puts "Good morning" }

If a method contains parameters, you should write them before the data block:

verbose.say("Mark", "manager") { puts "Good morning" }

Methods can invoke data blocks through a Ruby statement called "yield." Basically, "yield" is a statement that calls the data block linked to the method involved. The example given below will show you how "yield" statements work. In this example, you'll create a method twice. Then, you will call that method and put a data block right after it.

def sample_block

   puts "The starting point"

   yield

   yield

   puts "The endpoint"

end

   sample_block { puts "The midpoint" }

output:

The starting point

The midpoint

The midpoint

The endpoint

Chapter 3: Objects, Variables, and Classes

In this chapter, you'll know why programmers consider Ruby as an object-oriented programming language. You will also learn how to create your own objects, variables, and classes.

Let's start this chapter by solving a basic problem. Let's assume that you are the manager of a bookstore. You perform stock control each week. Clerks record books using portable scanners. These scanners create a basic CSV (i.e. comma-separated value) file that contains a row for every book. Each row contains the price and ISBN of the book. If you'll access one of these CSV files, you'll see values similar to these:

"ISBN", "Price"

"1-834672-45-6", 10.50

"1-213994-23-9", 25.99

"1-598447-99-4", 14.49

You need to check each CSV file and determine two pieces of information: (1) how many copies of each book you have; and (2) the total price of all the available books.

While you are designing an object-oriented system, you should always determine the stuff you're working on. In most cases, each kind of stuff turns into a class once your program is complete. Each "thing" is an instance of a class.

As you can see, you need to represent the data recorded by the portable scanners. The instances involved here represent one data row, and the totality of these Ruby objects represents all the information you've collected.

Let's use "Book_In_Stock" as the identifier of this class. Keep in mind that the name of a class begins with a capital letter. Here's the code that you need to type:

```
class Book_In_Stock

end
```

As you've seen in an earlier chapter, you may generate a new instance of a class using the "new" keyword:

```
first_book = Book_In_Stock.new

second_book = Book_In_Stock.new
```

Once you have executed this code, you will get two different objects from the Book_In_Stock class. However, the only difference between these objects is their respective name. These objects are almost identical. Additionally, these objects don't contain any data.

You can solve the problem stated above using the "initialize" method. This method allows you to set an object's state during the construction phase. You may store this information in an instance variable within the object. Since Ruby objects have their own group of variables, objects may have their own distinct state.

You can update the class definition this way:

```
class Book_In_Stock
  def initialize(isbn, amount)
    @isbn    =  isbn
    @amount  =  Float(amount)
  end
end
```

The "initialize" method is a special part of any Ruby application. Once you invoke Book_In_Stock.new to generate an object, Ruby will assign some memory space for that object. Then, Ruby will call the "initialize" method of the object and pass all of the parameters supplied to "new." That means you can write codes that set the state of your object.

For the Book_In_Stock class, "initialize" accepts two parameters. The parameters involved here are similar to the method's local variables. Thus, each parameter follows the naming convention of the said local variables. However, just like any local variable, a parameter will disappear once "initialize" returns, so you need to transfer it to an instance variable. This behavior is usual among initialize methods—its purpose is to ensure the usability of your object once "initialize" returns.

Lastly, this example shows a basic validation process. "Float" accepts an argument and turns it into a floating-point value. The program will stop in case the conversion process fails. In this process, you're telling Ruby that the object for "amount" must be convertible to floating-point data.

The Attributes

The objects you created inside Book_In_Stock possess a state (i.e. the price and the ISBN). This state is applicable only to those objects. This is an excellent feature in most cases. It means objects need to maintain their consistency.

Secretive objects, however, are completely useless – you may generate them but you can't use them. Normally, you'll create methods that allow you to access and modify an objects' state. Programmers use the term "attribute" when referring to a state that you can access from the "outside world."

For the objects inside Book_In_Stock, you need to know the price and ISBN of the available books. You can accomplish this by creating "accessor" methods:

```ruby
class BookInStock
  def initialize(isbn, price)
    @isbn = isbn
    @price = Float(price)
  end
  def isbn
    @isbn
  end
  def price
    @price
  end
  #  ..
end
```

```
book = BookInStock.new("isbn1", 12.34)
puts "ISBN    = #{book.isbn}"
puts "Price   = #{book.price}"
```
produces:
```
  ISBN   = isbn1
  Price  = 12.34
```

With this code, you'll create methods that can get the data of instance variables. For instance, isbn (a method) gets the data of @isbn (an instance variable).

The Writable Attributes

Some situations require you to set the attributes of an object from the outside. For instance, you need to reduce the total price of some books after analyzing the scan results.

In the Ruby language, you can access an object's attributes as if it's an ordinary variable. Thus, you can assign a value to a variable if you need to assign an attribute's value. You can complete this by defining a method that has "=" at the end of its name. You can use these methods as targets of assignment operations:

```
class BookInStock
  attr_reader :isbn, :price
  def initialize(isbn, price)
    @isbn  = isbn
    @price = Float(price)
  end
  def price=(new_price)
    @price = new_price
  end
  #  . . .
end

book = BookInStock.new("isbn1", 33.80)
puts "ISBN    = #{book.isbn}"
```

```
    puts "Price    = #{book.price}"
    book.price = book.price * 0.75          # discount price
produces:
    ISBN       = isbn1
    Price      = 33.8
    New price = 25.35
```

The assignment operation that begins with "book.price" calls the "price=" method inside the object called "book." This operation will pass reduced prices as arguments. When you write a method that has "=" at the end of its name, you may place that name on the left-hand side of the expression.

Keep in mind that you can use a shortcut to create basic attribute-setting Ruby methods. You may use the "attr_writer" to create write-only accessors. However, you'll rarely use this option. Since you will likely need reading and writing capabilities, you should use the method called "attr_accessor". Here's an example:

```
  class BookInStock
    attr_reader   :isbn
    attr_accessor :price
    def initiealize(isbn, price)
      @isbn  = isbn
      @price = Float(price)
    end
    #  ...
  end
    book = BookInStock.new("isbn1", 33.80)
    puts "ISBN    = #{book.isbn}"
    puts "Price   = #{book.price}"
    book.price = book.price * 0.75          # discount price
produces:
    ISBN       = isbn1
    Price      = 33.8
    New price = 25.35
```

Access Control

While defining class interfaces, you should think about how you'll expose those classes to the external world. Excessive access to a class can result to program "coupling"—users will rely on the information available in the implementation of your class, instead of the logical interface. Fortunately, the simplest way to alter the state of a Ruby object is by invoking a method linked to it. That means you can control access to an object by controlling the access to its methods. As a general rule, you should never expose any method that may compromise your objects.

Here are the three levels of protection offered by Ruby:

- Private – You can't call private methods using explicit receivers. To call a private method, you need to be in the current object's context. Thus, you can't invoke the private methods of another object.

- Protected – To invoke a protected method, you need to use an object from the class itself or its subclasses. Access to methods is passed on to inheriting classes.

- Public – This access control allows anyone to call the method. By default, almost all of the methods in Ruby are tagged as public.

How to Set the Access Control of a Method

Ruby allows you to specify the access level of a method inside a module or class definition. You just have to use the "access functions" of this language, namely: private, protected and public.

If you won't add any argument, these functions will affect the access control of the methods you'll create in the future. C++ and Java programmers may be familiar with this behavior.

Check the example below:

```
class MyClass
   def method1    # default is 'public'
     # . . .
   end
  protected        # subsequent methods will be 'protected'
   def method2    # will be 'protected'
     # . . .
   end
  private          # subsequent methods will be 'private '
   def method3    # will be 'private'
     # . . .
   end
  public           # subsequent methods will be 'public'
   def method4    # will be 'public'
     # . . .
   end
end
```

The Variables

After learning how to create an object, you need to know how to retain objects. In Ruby, you need to use variables to track the objects you created. The code given below will illustrate this idea:

book = "dictionary"

puts "In this example, 'book' belongs to the #{book.class} data type"

puts "Its ID is #{book.object_id}

puts "Its value, on the other hand, is '#{book}'"

output:

In this example, 'book' belongs to the String data type

Its ID is 999

Its value, on the other hand, is 'dictionary'

The first line of this code generates a string object and assigns "dictionary" as its initial value. Then, it created a variable named "book.object_id" – this variable points to the new object. If you'll analyze this example, you'll see that the variable is indeed a string. It has an ID, a value, and a class.

In Ruby, variables are not objects. Rather, variables are references to existing objects. You use variables to point to objects that are "floating" inside the system.

Chapter 4: Collections of Data

Almost all programs involve collections of information. This programming language offers two pre-installed classes to take care of these collections. These classes are known as hashes and arrays. You need to master these special classes if you want to become a skilled Ruby user. Mastering these classes isn't easy, since they involve large interfaces.

Aside from hashes and classes, Ruby has one more feature designed for handling collections of data. This feature, which is the "block syntax," allows you to encapsulate blocks of code. If you'll use these "blocks" with a collection of data, they become effective iterator constructs.

This chapter will explain how hashes and arrays work. Additionally, it will teach you how to use the block syntax and iterator constructs.

Arrays

The "Array" class contains object references. Each reference takes up a spot inside the array. You can identify a reference using an integer index.

Ruby allows you to generate arrays through literals or by creating objects in the "Array" class. Literal arrays are objects you'll list between a pair of square brackets. The code given below will help you understand this idea:

```
x = [ 44, "basketball", 99.99 ]

x.class   #   Array

x.length  #   3

x[0]    #   44

x[1]    #   "basketball"

x[2]    #   99.99

x[5]    #   nil


y = Array.new

y.class   #   Array

y.length  #   0

y[0]    # → "sample"

y[1]    # → "array"

y    # → ["sample", "array"]
```

You should use square brackets (i.e. []) to index an array. Just like other operators in this language, "[]" is a method that you can override within subclasses. The index of an array always begins with zero. If you will use non-negative integers as indices, you will get an object (if an object exists in the specified position) or "nil" (if the position doesn't hold any object). The index will work backwards if you will enter a negative number. Check the following example:

$x = [10, 20, 30, 40, 50]$

$x[-1]$ # → 50

$x[-5]$ # → 10

$x[-47]$ # → nil

You may also index an array using number pairs. The format that you should use is "[starting point, count]". With this approach, you will create an array that contains the objects specified in the format. Here's an example:

$x = [10, 20, 30, 40, 50]$

$x[1, 2]$ # → [20, 30]

$x[2, 1]$ # → [30]

Hashes

A "hash" (also called "map," "dictionary", or "associative array") is similar to an array in that it is an indexed set of references. The main difference between these collections is that an array requires integers as indexes, whereas a hash can take any data type (e.g. string) as an index. Each item inside a hash involves two objects: (1) the index (also known as the key) and (2) the data to be saved inside the index. To retrieve an entry, you just have to index the hash through the key you entered previously.

The code given below contains hash literals. Again, hash literals are key/value pairs written between a pair of curly braces.

x = { 'pen' => 'writer' , 'camera' => 'photographer' , 'brush' => 'painter' }

x.length   # → 3

x['pen']   # → "writer"

x['brush']   # → "painter"

x[10]   = 'poet'

x['knife']   = butcher

x   # → {"pen"→"writer", "camera"→"photographer", "brush"→"painter",

*   10→"poet", "knife"→"butcher"}*

This example uses strings as hash keys. If you want to use symbols instead of strings, you may use either the modern syntax (i.e. key:value) or the traditional one (i.e. the one that begins with =>). Check the following codes:

x = { pen: 'writer', camera: 'photographer', brush: 'painter' }

 # This statement and the one given below produce the same results.

x = { :pen => 'writer', :camera => 'photographer', :brush => 'painter' }

Compared with an array, a hash has one major advantage: it accepts any object from any data type. Additionally, the Ruby language takes note of the arrangement of items inside a hash. Once you check these items, Ruby will present them using the same order or arrangement.

Data Blocks

A data block is just a piece of code placed between a pair of braces or the "do" and "end" keywords. These forms are almost identical. The main difference between these forms lies in operational precedence (you'll learn about this later). In general, the Ruby language prefers braces for single-line blocks and do/end for multi-line blocks. Analyze the following example:

*sample_array.each { |sample_value| puts sample_value * 5 }*

sum = 1

second_array.each do |sample_value|

  sum += sample_value

  puts sample_value / sum

end

A block has some similarities with the content of a method. Similar to a method, a data block may accept one or more parameters. Both of the data blocks given above accept one parameter (i.e. sample_value). Additionally, a block's body won't run when the interpreter sees it. Rather, the language will just store the block for future use. This feature also applies to methods.

You need to place data blocks in your Ruby codes right after a method's invocation. If that method accepts parameters, the data block will appear after the said parameters. This is the reason why some programmers think of data blocks as "extra parameters."

The Iterators

Basically, iterators are methods that can call code blocks.

When you call a code block, the language treats it as an actual method and applies the "yield" command on it. Whenever you execute "yield", you'll invoke the code block you're working on. The following code will help you understand this concept:

def repeat_twice

  yield

  yield

end

repeat_twice { puts "I'm awesome." }

output:

I'm awesome.

I'm awesome.

I'm awesome.

The code block (i.e. the statements inside the curly braces) are linked to the invocation to the repeat_twice method. Inside this method, the "yield" command will run twice. Whenever "yield" runs, it also invokes the statements inside the code block.

Chapter 5: The Sharing Functionalities of Ruby

This chapter will teach you two mechanisms that help you share data between different classes. Read this material carefully, as data sharing is an important aspect of computer programming.

Class Inheritance

The "puts" method uses the "to_s" method of an object to convert objects into strings. However, there are some classes that don't have to_s. Regardless of this fact, the objects inside these classes react properly whenever you invoke to_s. This functionality is related with subclassing, inheritance, and how the language chooses which method to execute once you send messages to a Ruby object.

Inheritance lets you generate classes that are specialized areas of an existing class. The original class is called the "parent" while the class (or classes) under it is known as the "child" (or "children").

Subclassing is a mechanism that can be understood easily. In this mechanism, the "child" class inherits the properties of the parent. That means the instance methods of the parent will also exist inside the child.

Let's work on a basic example. This example will become more complex as you read the rest of this section. The definition of the parent class and its child is:

```ruby
class Parent
  def say_hello
    puts "Hello from #{self}"
  end
end
p = Parent.new
p.say_hello
# Subclass the parent . . .
class Child < Parent
end
c = Child.new
c.say._hello
```
produces:
```
Hello from #<Parent:0x0a40c4>
Hello from  #<Child:0x0a3d68>
```

The parent contains a method (i.e. say_hello). You invoked that method by generating another instance of the "Parent" class and saved an object that points to the said instance. You stored the reference in a variable called "p."

Then, you used "<" to generate a subclass. The "<" symbol informs Ruby that you want to create a child class. Here, you should specify the name of the parent class on the right-hand side of the symbol.

As you can see, the subclass didn't define a method. But then, when you created its instance, you were able to invoke "say_hello." This invocation became possible because a child class gets a copy of the methods inside its parent.

To identify a child's parent class, you just need to use the method called "superclass." Check the following code:

```
class Parent

end
class Child < Parent
end
puts "The superclass of Child is #{Child.superclass}"
```
produces:
```
  The superclass of Child is Parent
```

To get the "parent" of a parent class, you may run the following code:

```
  class Parent
  end
  puts "The superclass of Parent is #{Parent.superclass}"
```
produces:
```
  The superclass of Parent is Object
```

A special class called "BasicObject" serves as the "root" of Ruby's class hierarchy. You may access any class inside a Ruby program, identify the parent of that class, then the parent of that parent class, etc. If you'll keep on doing this, you'll reach the BasicObject class of your program.

If you'll invoke a method that doesn't exist in a subclass, the language will check the parent. If the parent doesn't have the method you called, Ruby will go up the class hierarchy until there's no class to check.

The Modules

You can use a module to group classes, constants, and methods together. In general, a module offers the following benefits:

- they give you namespaces and stop name-related conflicts
- they offer a facility called "mixin"

The Namespaces

While writing complex Ruby applications, you will surely create reusable code blocks—collections of related processes that you can apply on other objects. You may break these code blocks into small files so that you can share the processes among various Ruby applications.

Typically, programmers organize these code blocks into classes. These people save one or more classes inside a file. Some situations, however, require you to combine different kinds of objects inside a class.

If you're looking for a simple approach, you may save all these objects in a single file and use the resulting file on any application that requires it. C programmers are familiar with this technique. However, this technique has a weakness. Let's assume that you created a collection of "natural elements" (i.e. air, water, fire and earth). You stored these elements in a file called "elements.rb" so you can use them in the future. Meanwhile, your sister coded the basic necessities of human beings (e.g. air, food, shelter, etc.). She saved it in a file named "basic.rb".Then, your brother decided to create a program that specifies the elements required by humans. He needs to use both elements.rb and basic.rb to complete his application. However, there's a problem: both of these programs contain an object named "air".

You can solve this problem using a "module." A module defines a namespace (i.e. a virtual place where constants and methods can exist without affecting other Ruby objects). That means you can save the natural elements in a module. Then, save the basic necessities inside another module.

The naming convention for classes also applies to modules: the first letter should be capitalized. Also, the definition for a module's method is similar to that of a typical method.

You can load the resulting files into an application using the "require" command. If you want to reference "air" unambiguously, your code may qualify that method by checking the name of its container (i.e. the module). Here, you'll just add two colons after the module's name.

The Mixins

Mixins are functions of a module. With mixins, you won't have to deal with parent-child relationships in your programs anymore.

The previous section taught you how to define the methods of a module. The name of the module comes before that of the method. This function is similar to that of class methods, so you're probably thinking about defining one or more instance methods inside a module. Well, modules aren't classes so they can't have any instance. However, Ruby allows you to include modules in your class definitions. With this option, even classes can access the instance methods of a module. These objects are mixed in. Actually, mixed modules act as parent classes.

Check the following code:

```
module Debug
  def who_am_i?
    "#{self.class.name }"  (\##{self.object_id}): #{self.to_s}"
  end
end
class Phonograph
  include Debug
  # ...
end
class EightTrack
  include Debug
  # ...
end
ph = Phonograph.new("West End Blues")
et = EightTrack.new("Surrealistic Pillow")

ph.who:am_i?  # =>  "Phonograph (#330450): West End Blues"
et.who:am_i?  # =>  "EightTrack (#330420): Surrealistic Pillow"
```

Since you included the module called "Debug", the two classes (i.e. EightTrack and Phonograph) can access the instance method named "who_am_i?".

Chapter 6: The Standard Data Types

The programs you have seen so far involved procs, hashes, and arrays. You haven't learned enough information about the basic data types of the Ruby language. These data types are: strings, ranges, regular expressions and numbers. This chapter will focus on strings, ranges, and numbers. You'll learn about regular expressions in the next chapter.

The Strings

Basically, a string is a group of characters. A string normally contains printable characters; however, this is not mandatory. You may also place binary information inside a string. In addition, each string belongs to the "String" class.

Most programmers create a string using a string literal (i.e. a set of characters placed inside a pair of delimiters). Since representing binary data is difficult, string literals can accept different escape sequences. Ruby will replace these escape sequences with the right binary values during the compilation phase. The level of substitution that will occur depends on the delimiter used. If you'll use single quotes, two backslashes will become one ordinary backslash. A backslash and a double quote, on the other hand, becomes a double quote.

Here are some examples:

'You can use "\\" to escape characters.'   *# → You can use "\" to escape characters.*

'Today, is a great day to say \"Hello, world!\" # → Today is a great day to say "Hello, world!"

In Ruby, double-quoted strings offer more escape codes than single-quoted ones. One of the most popular ones is \n, the escape sequence for a newline character. Additionally, you may use the #{expression}sequence to convert code values into strings. If you're dealing with instance, class, or global variables, the curly braces are not mandatory. Check the following statements:

"Each day consists of #{60*60*24} seconds" # → Each day consists of 86400 seconds

"The cannon sounded #{'Boom! ' *3}"   # → The cannon sounded Boom! Boom! Boom!

Encodings

In the latest versions of Ruby, each string has its own encoding. The encoding of a source file affects the encoding of all the string literals inside it. If an explicit encoding doesn't exist, source files (and the strings inside them) will use the US-ASCII encoding.

sample_string = "dinosaur"

puts   "The   encoding   of   #{sample_string}   is #{sample_string.encoding}"

output:

The encoding of "dinosaur" is US-ASCII

57

The Ranges

In Ruby, ranges can help you implement three different functionalities: intervals, sequences, and conditions. Let's discuss these functionalities in detail:

How to Use a Range as an Interval

Programmers use ranges as interval tests. Here, the programmers check whether a value belongs to an interval the range represents. This process requires the "===" operator. Analyze these expressions:

(3..7)   === 4   # This expression evaluates to true.

(3..7)   === 2   # This expression evaluates to false.

(3..7)   === 6.99 # This expression evaluates to true.

('e'..'i') === 'g' # This expression evaluates to true.

('e'..'i') === 'j'   # This expression evaluates to false.

How to Use a Range as a Sequence

Programmers consider this as the most natural method of using ranges. A sequence has a starting point and an endpoint. It also has the ability to generate successive values. In the Ruby language, you need to use the "..." operator or the ".." operator when creating a sequence. You can use the three-dot variant to generate ranges that exclude the highest value. The two-dot variant, on the other hand, generates ranges that include all of the values involved. Here are some examples:

'e'..'x'

3..7

1..."dinosaur".length

Ruby allows you to convert ranges into arrays using "to_a". Alternatively, you may convert arrays into enumerators using "to_enum". The statements given below will illustrate this:

(3..7).to_a   # → [3, 4, 5, 6, 7]

('abc'..'abe').to_a   # → ["abc", "abd", "abe"]

enum = ('abc'..'abe').to_enum

enum.next   # This will give you "abc"

enum.next   # This will give you "abd"

How to Use a Range as a Condition

You may also use a range as a conditional expression. With this option, a range will behave like a toggle switch – it will turn on if the first condition is true, and turn off if the second condition is true. For instance, the code given below prints several lines from the standard input. The initial line of each set has "start" in it. The final line, however, has "end."

```
while line = gets
  puts line if line =~ /start/ .. line =~ /end/
end
```

The Numbers

This computer language offers different kinds of numbers, namely: integers, rational numbers, complex numbers, and floating-point numbers. An integer can have any length (your computer's available memory determines the maximum digits an integer can have). If you are dealing with integers inside a particular range, Ruby will store the integers as binary values. These integers also belong to the "Fixnum" class. Integers that belong to that range will go to a class called "Bignum". This is a transparent process. Additionally, Ruby will handle all of the data conversions on your behalf.

Check the following code:

```
num = 81
6.times do
  puts "#{num.class}: #{num}"
  num *= num
end
produces>
  Fixnum: 81
  Fixnum: 6561
  Fixnum: 43046721
  Bignum: 1853020188851841
  Bignum: 3433683820292512484657849089281
  Bignum: 11790184577738583171520872861412518665678211592275841109
096961
```

While writing an integer, you need to use a leading sign, a base indicator, and one or more digits that belong to the right base. You may use underscores to divide long integers into manageable bits. If you'll divide integers this way, the system will ignore all of the underscore characters.

Here are some examples:

234   => *234*   *# It belongs to the Fixnum class.*

0d234   => *234*   *# It belongs to the Fixnum class.*

23_4   => *234*   *# It belongs to the Fixnum class.*

-987   =>   *-987*   *# This negative integer belongs to the Fixnum class.*

Numeric literals that contain an exponent and/or a decimal point becomes a "Float" value, which is the equivalent of "Double" in other languages (e.g. C#). Make sure that the decimal point is placed between two numbers. If a letter comes after the decimal point (e.g. 3.e5), Ruby will think that the letter is a method that must be invoked on the number.

In the latest versions of Ruby, the support for complex and rational numbers is already set in the language interpreter. A complex number represents a point within the so-called "complex plane." Each complex number consists of two parts: the "real" part and the "imaginary" part. A rational number, on the other hand, is the ratio you'll get from two fractional numbers. Thus, rational numbers have exact representations.

There's no syntax for writing complex and rational numbers. Rather, you'll write them by invoking two constructor methods (i.e. "Complex" and "Rational") explicitly.

Chapter 7: The Regular Expressions

Regular expressions are patterns that you can compare with strings. These patterns can be basic or complex. Here are the major benefits offered by regular expressions:

- You may test strings to find out whether they match any pattern.

- You may pull a whole string (or some parts of it) that matches a pattern.

- You may alter strings. Ruby allows you to modify the sections that match the pattern you used.

This language offers complete support for regular expressions. That means you can quickly and conveniently perform pattern comparisons and/or substitutions. In this part of the book, you'll learn about the fundamentals of expression patterns. You will also discover how the language implements matching and/or replacing processes through those patterns.

Ruby and Its Regular Expressions

You can create regular expressions in different ways. Currently, the most popular technique involves writing the regular expression between two forward slashes. That means /dinosaur/, /chess/, and /basketball/ are valid samples of regular expression literals.

A pattern literal is similar to a double-quoted string. Particularly, you may perform substitutions in your patterns using "#{...}".

How to Match Strings and Patterns

In Ruby, you need to match strings against patterns using the "=~" operator. This operator shows the point where the match happened:

/run/ =~ "hit and run"   *# → 8*

/run/ =~ "runner"   *# → 0*

/run/ =~ 'RUN'   *# → nil*

You may rewrite these statements this way:

"hit and run" =~ /run/   *# → 8*

"runner" =~ /run/   *# → 0*

"RUN" =~ /run/   *# → nil*

Since this process gives you "nil" if no match exists and "nil" is treated as false", you may use the output of this process for your conditional statements. Here is an example:

str = "hit and run"

if str =~ /run/

   puts "I want to run towards the finish line"

end

output:

I want to run towards the finish line

How to Use a Pattern to Change a String

In the Ruby language, "sub" is a method that accepts patterns and replacement texts. If this method locates a match, it will delete the matched item and enter the assigned text. The example given below will illustrate this concept:

first_sample = "hit and run"

second_sample = first_sample.sub(/hit/, "laugh")

puts "I was involved in a #{second_sample} incident."

output:

I was involved in a laugh and run incident.

The effect of this method only applies to the initial match. If you want to replace all of the matches in your code, use the "gsub" method instead. Here's an example:

first_sample = "hit and run"

second_sample = first_sample.sub(/n/, "$")

third_sample = first_sample.gsub(/n/, "$")

puts "This line uses the sub method: #{second_sample}"

puts "This line uses the gsub method: #{third_sample}"

output:

This line uses the sub method: hit a$d run

This line uses the gsub method: hit a$d ru$

Pattern-Based Substitutions

You've learned how to perform string replacements using the sub/gsub methods. The examples given earlier involved fixed text. However, it's important to point out that substitution processes also work on other patterns (e.g. those that involve   groupings, alterations and/or alternations). Analyze the following code:

x = "the blue sky"

x.sub(/[aeiou]/, '!')   # →   "th! blue sky"

x.gsub(/aeiou]/, '!')   # →   "th! bl!! sky"

x.sub(/\s\S+/, ' ')   # →   "the sky"

x.gsub(/\s\S+/, ' ')   # →   "the"

The substitution methods accept a block or a string. If you used a block, Ruby will pass it to the substring that matches it. Then, the value of your block will replace that of the first string.

x = "the blue sky"

x.sub(/[aeiou]/) { |vowel| vowel.upcase }   # → "thE blue sky"

xgsub(/[aeiou]/) { |vowel| vowel.upcase }   # → "thE blUE sky"

66

Let's assume that you need to normalize the names entered into an online program. It's possible that the users entered "john doe", "JOHN DOE", or "JoHN dOe", and you want to convert it to "John Doe". The method you'll see below is a basic iteration. It uses the \b\w pattern to match a word's initial character. You can work on all of the names quickly by combining \b\w with gsub. Here's the code:


```
def sample_case(names)

  names.downcase.gsub(/\b\w/) {|first| first.upcase }

end
```


```
sample_case("john doe")    # →    "John Doe"

sample_case("JOHN DOE")  # →    "John Doe"

sample_case("JoHN dOe")  # →    "John Doe"
```

Chapter 8: The Methods of the Ruby Language

The chapters you've read so far defined and used various methods. However, to keep the lessons simple, important details regarding Ruby methods were not given. In this chapter, you'll learn all you need to know about Ruby's methods.

How to Define a Method

As you've seen from the previous example, you need to use the "def" keyword to define a method. The name of a method must always start with an underscore or a letter. You may add "=", "!", or "?" at the end of a method's name. When defining a method that produces Boolean results, most programmers add a question mark at the end of that method's name. Here are some examples:

5.odd?   # → true

6.odd?   # → false

You may place an exclamation mark at the end of the name of a "dangerous method" (i.e. a method that can modify its receiver). Programmers refer to a dangerous method as a "bang method." For example, the String class offers the "chop" method and the "chop!" method. The former gives you an altered string, whereas the latter alters the receiver you assigned.

After setting the name of your method, you must declare one or more parameters for it. A parameter is a local variable that you need to write between parentheses. Check the following code:

```
def   sample_method(argument1,   argument2,   argument3,
argument4) # four arguments

   # You need to type the method's code here.

end

def another_method   # zero arguments

   # You need to type the method's code here.

end
```

The Ruby language allows you to set the default values of your arguments. To accomplish this, you just have to type "=" and the appropriate Ruby expression. This expression may contain references to arguments you've already listed:

```
def                    sample_method(argument1="Tennis",
argument2="Basketball", argument3 ="Soccer")

   "#{argument1}, #{argument2}, #{argument3}"

end
```

```
sample_method          # → "Tennis, Basketball, Soccer"

sample_method("Karate")               # → "Karate, Basketball,
Soccer"

sample_method("Karate", "Kung Fu")        # → "Karate, Kung
Fu, Soccer"

sample_method("Karate", "Kung Fu", "Boxing"   # → "Karate,
Kung Fu, Boxing"
```

Argument Lists

In some cases, you need to pass varying numbers of arguments or store different arguments into one parameter. To do these things, you just have to place a "*" before entering the parameter's name. Programmers refer to this process as "argument splatting." Check the following code:

```
def varargs(arg1, *rest)
  "arg1=#{arg1}.    rest=#{rest.inspect}"
end

varargs("one")                 # =>  arg1=one.  rest=[]
varargs("one", "two")          # =>  arg1=one.  rest=[two]
varargs "one", "two", "three"  # =>  arg1=one.  rest=[two, three]
```

Here, you assigned the initial argument to the initial method. Then, you set an asterisk as the prefix of the second parameter. Because of this, Ruby bundled the rest of the arguments into an array object.

Some programmers utilize the "*" symbol to indicate arguments that the method doesn't use. In the example given below, you'll invoke "super" without giving any parameter. Basically, you called the method inside the parent class, giving it the parameters you assigned to the actual method.

```
class Child < Parent
...def do_something(*not_used)
    # our processing
    super
  end
end
```

Invoking a Method

Invoking a method involves one mandatory step and three optional steps. The mandatory step mentioned here is the process of specifying the method's name. The optional steps, however, are (1) the specification of a receiver, (2) the insertion of a block, and (3) the passing of parameters.

The following method has all of the steps discussed above:

connection.game("DOTA2") {|p| show_progress(p) }

Here, "connection" serves as the receiver, "game" is the method's identifier, "DOTA2" acts as the parameter, and the code snippet between the curly braces serves as the block. While calling this method, Ruby assigns "self" to "connection" and runs the method inside that object. When it comes to module and class methods, the name of the module or the class will be the receiver.

How to Pass a Parameter to Your Method

Each parameter follows the name of the method it belongs to. If your code isn't confusing, you may remove the parentheses that enclose your arguments. This approach won't affect the output or behavior of your Ruby program. However, if you are dealing with long and/or complicated codes, it would be best if you'll retain the said parentheses. Here's a basic rule: if you're not sure, leave the parentheses alone.

x = obj.sample_hash   # This line and the one below it produce identical results.

x = obj.samplehash()

obj.sample_method "Argument1", argument2, argument3 # The output of this line is similar

obj.sample_method ("Argument1", argument2, argument3) # to this one.

The Outputs of a Method

Methods return a value when you invoke them. However, Ruby doesn't require you to use the resulting values. A method's value is identical to that of the final statement it performed. Analyze the following code:

def first_method

  "first"

end

first_method   # → "first"

def second_method(sample_argument)

  case

  when sample_argument < 0 then "The value is positive"

  when sample_argument > 0 then "The value is negative"

  else   "The value is equal to zero"

  end

end

72

second_method(99)   # → *"The value is positive"*

second_method(-45)   # → *"The value is negative"*

The Ruby language supports "return", a statement that allows you to exit the current method. This statement takes arguments. To determine the value of "return", you just have to add all of the values of the arguments assigned to it.

The example given below shows you how to use the "return" statement. Here, "return" terminates the loop within a method. Here's the code:


```ruby
def meth_three
  100.times do |num|
    square = num+num
    return num, square if square > 1000
  end
end
meth_three    # => [32, 1024]
```

Chapter 9: Ruby Expressions

The expressions you've seen so far are pretty basic. Some of those expressions are actually simpler than "x + y = z". It's important to note that you can create functional Ruby programs without studying this particular chapter. However, the capabilities of your programs will be extremely limited.

A distinct characteristic of the Ruby language is that it treats almost everything as an expression. For example, Ruby allows you to link different statements:

$x = y = z = 1$ $\# \rightarrow 1$

$[\ 9, 1, 5, 6\ ].sort.reverse$ $\# \rightarrow [9, 6, 5, 1]$

Additionally, the "typical statements" of C and Java are considered as expressions in the Ruby language. For instance, the value returned by "if" statements is identical to that of the final expression they executed. Check the following code snippet:

```
song_type = if song.mp3_type == MP3::Jazz
              if song.written < Date.new(1935, 1,1 1)
                 Song::TradJazz
              else
                 Song::Jazz
              end
            else
              Song::Other
            End
rating = case votes_cast
              when 0 . . . 10    then Rating::SkipThisOne
              when 10 . . . 50   then Rating::CouldDoBetter
              else                   Rating::Rave
              end
```

Expressions that Involve Operators

This language has the typical operators (e.g. -, +, %, etc.) and some surprises. You'll learn about the Ruby operators in a later chapter.

You should remember that Ruby implements operators as method invocations. For instance, if you'll type x / y − z, you are requiring "a" (or the object it points to) to run the "/" method, adding "y" as the second parameter. Then, you tell Ruby to run "+" using the result of the previous operation and the value of "c". If you'll convert this into actual Ruby statements, you'll get the following:

$x, y, z = 20, 5, 2$

$x / y - z$ # → 2

$(x./(y)).-(z)$ # → 2

Since Ruby treats everything as an object and you may redefine any instance method, you have the option to redefine arithmetic expressions if you're not happy with the results you're receiving.

Moreover, your own classes are similar to built-in objects in that they can get involved in "operational expressions." For instance, the << operator lets you append objects to the recipient. You can use this feature on arrays:

$x = [3, 4, 5]$

$x << 6$ # → [3, 4, 5, 6]

You may also use this on the classes you created:

```
class ScoreKeeper
  def initialize
    @total_score = 0
    @count = 0
  end
  def <<(score)
    @total_score += score
    @count +=1
    self
  end

      def average
        fail "No scores" if @count == 0
        Float(@total_score) / @count
      end
    end
    scores = ScoreKeeper.new
    scores << 10 << 20 << 40
    puts "Average = #{scores.average}"
produces:
    Average = 23.3333333333333
```

This code has a subtle aspect: the "<<" operator returns the "self" object explicitly. This behavior allows the chain of methods to run. Since "<<" gives you the object named "scores" whenever you call the former, you may invoke it again to pass another score.

Just like <<, *, and +, Ruby treats "square-bracket indexing" as a call for a method. If you'll enter:

sample_object[3, 4, 5]

you're invoking a method called "[]" on "sample_object".

Additionally, you are passing three parameters on the same object. To create this method, you may enter:

```
class  SampleClass
   def [] (param1, param2, param3)
     # ...
     end
end
```

The Miscellaneous Expression

Aside from method calls, statement expressions, and operator expressions, the Ruby language offers another element that you may incorporate into your expressions.

Expanding a Command

If you'll type a string between a pair of "backticks" (i.e. `` ` ``), that string will run as if it's an actual command. You can also activate this feature by adding "%x" at the beginning of the string. The result of the command is identical to the expression's value. Ruby won't eliminate newline characters, so the resulting value might have a linefeed or return character. Here are some examples:

```
`date`          # → "Tue April 26 11:10:35 EST 2016\n"

%x{echo "I'm awesome"}    # → "I'm awesome\n"
```

Assignment Expressions

Almost all of the examples included in this book involve assignment. In this part of the book, you'll learn about the most important aspects of assignment expressions.

Basically, an assignment expression assigns the "lvalue" (i.e. the attribute or variable found on the left-hand side of the equal sign) to the "rvalue" (i.e. the value found on the right-hand side of the equal sign). The "rvalue" serves as the output of this procedure. Ruby allows you to chain multiple assignment expressions or assign values in unexpected situations. Check the following examples:

$x = y = 5 + 5 + 2$

$x \quad \# \rightarrow 12$

$y \quad \# \rightarrow 12$

$x = (y = 5 + 5) \, 2$

$x \quad \# \rightarrow 12$

$y \quad \# \rightarrow 10$

This programming language supports two types of assignment expressions. The first type sets a reference to an existing constant or variable. This kind of assignment expression is a built-in feature of Ruby. The code given below shows how you can use this assignment expression:

singer = "Charlie Puth"

favorite_number = 23

The second type requires an element reference or object attribute on the equal sign's left-hand side. This is a special type since you'll implement it by invoking a method on the lvalue. Consequently, you may override this type of assignment expression.

You've already learned how to create writable attributes. You just need to specify the name of your method and add the "=" symbol. The parameter will serve as the rvalue of the assignment expression. Additionally, you already know how to define square brackets as methods. The code given below will serve as a reviewer:

```
class ProjectList
  def initialize
    @projects = []
  end
  def projects=(list)
    @projects = list.map(&:upcase)   # store list of names in uppercase
  end
  def [](offset)
    @projects[offset]
  end
end

list = ProjectList.new
list.projects = %w{ strip sand prime sand paint sand paint rub paint }
list[3]   # =>   "SAND"
list[4]   # =>   "PAINT"
```

As you can see from this example, the methods that set attributes don't need to match the instance variables. Additionally, attribute writers may exist without any attribute reader, and vice versa.

Parallel Assignment Operations

Most computer languages require codes to switch the values of two variables. Here is an example:

int x = 3;

int y = 4;

int sample;

sample = x;

x = y;

y = sample;

In the Ruby language, you can accomplish this quickly and easily:

x = 3

y = 4

x, y = y, x

Ruby allows you to list multiple rvalues—you just have to separate the entries using commas. As soon as the language notices multiple rvalues, it will activate a function called "parallel assignment." Programmers divide "parallel assignment" into two steps. These steps are:

1. The language will evaluate the rvalues and store them in an array. The resulting array will serve as the output of the

assignment operation.

2. Ruby will inspect the left-hand side of the expression. If it consists of one element, the array obtained from the previous step will go that element.

Here's an example:

$x = [\,3, 4, 5, 6\,]$ $\# \rightarrow x = [3, 4, 5, 6]$

$y = [\,3, 4, 5, 6\,]$ $\# \rightarrow y = [3, 4, 5, 6]$

If your code has multiple lvalues, Ruby will match those against the rvalues of the same expression. If the number of items doesn't match, excess items will be deleted. This rule also applies to an lvalue that has a comma. The example given below will illustrate this idea:

$x, y = 3, 4, 5, 6$ $\# x{=}3, y{=}4$

$z, = 10, 20, 30$ $\# z{=}10$

Asterisks and Assignment Operations

If the right-hand side of your assignment expression has an asterisk (also known as "splat"), Ruby will expand the rvalues into their constituents. This expansion will occur while Ruby evaluates the rvalues (before the actual assignment operation begins). Here's an example:

$x, y, z = *(3..4), 5$ # → $x = 3, y = 4, z = 5$

Only one lvalue can become a splat. That means an lvalue is extremely greedy—it will become an array and hold all of the rvalues it can access). Thus, if your final lvalue is a splat, it will consume all of the unassigned rvalues in the expression. The following code will illustrate this:

$x, *y = 3, 4, 5$ # → $x = 3, y = [4, 5]$

$x, *y = 3$ # → $x = 3, y = []$

The Nested Assignments

The left-hand side of your assignment expression may have a parenthesized collection of items. Ruby will treat these items as nested assignment expressions. Basically, Ruby will pull the matching rvalue and assign that to the listed items before processing the rest of the code. Here's an example:

$x, (y, z) = 3, 4, 5$ # → $x = 3, y = 4, z = nil$

$x, (y, z) = [3, 4, 5]$ # → $x = 3, y = 4, z = nil$

$x, (y, z) = 3, [4, 5]$ # → $x = 3, y = 4, z = 5$

$x, (y, z) = 3, [4, 5, 6, 7]$ # → $x = 3, y = 4, z = 5$

Other Types of Assignment Expressions

Just like other programming languages, Ruby offers syntactic shortcuts. For example, you may rewrite "x = x + 10" as "x += 10". Ruby uses an internal mechanism to convert the second syntax into the first one. Thus, any operator you defined as a method works as it should:


```
class Bowdlerize
  def initialize(string)
    @value = string.gsub(/[aeiou]/, '*')
  end
  def +(other)
    Bowdlerize.new(self.to_s + other.to_s)
  end
  def to_s
    @value
  end
end

a = Bowdlerize.new("damn ")  # =>  d*mn
a += "shame"                 # =>  d*mn sh*m*
```


Important Note: Ruby doesn't support the "autodecrement" (i.e. --) and "autoincrement" (i.e. ++) operators. While writing Ruby codes, you need to use "-=" and "+=" instead.

How to Execute Codes Conditionally

Ruby offers several mechanisms that you can use to execute codes conditionally. Most of these mechanisms are also available in other programming languages. Some of them, however, have distinct twists. Prior to discussing conditional expressions, you should study Boolean statements first.

The Boolean Statements

This language defines "truth" in a basic way. A value is true if it is not "false" or "nil." Thus, 0, 100, "dinosaur", and ":x_game" are true.

Since "nil" is equivalent to "false", conditional expressions in Ruby are easy and convenient. Here's an example:

```
While line = gets
  # process line
end
```

People who have used C, C++, and/or Perl experience problems in some cases. These problems are usually related with "zero." As a Ruby programmer, you need to keep in mind that "zero" is different from "false." Additionally, a strength whose length is zero doesn't evaluate to false. If you'll forget about these basic rules, your programs will produce errors.

Or, And, and Not

Ruby offers all of the traditional Boolean operators. Here, both the "&&" operator and the "and" keyword give their initial argument if that evaluates to false. If this is not the case, Ruby will assess and return the second argument. Programmers use the term "short-circuit evaluation" when referring to this kind of behavior. Keep in mind that "and" and "&&" are almost identical. The only significant difference between these operators is precedence.

nil %% 1   # → nil

"dinosaur" && 1   # → 1

false && 1   # → false

As you can see, "and" and "&&" will give you "true" only if the two arguments you specified are true.

In the same way, "or" and "||" will give their initial argument if it is true. If that argument is "false", these operators will inspect and process the other argument.

"dinosaur" || 1 # → "dinosaur"

nil || 1   # → 1

false || 1   # → 1

The Basics of "defined?"

In Ruby, "defined?" is an operator that gives nil if you didn't define its argument. If you defined the argument, this operator will simply describe that argument. It's important to point out that "defined?" accepts arbitrary expressions as arguments.

Here are some examples:

defined? Number   # → *"constant"*

defined? 50   # → *"expression"*

defined? x = 3   # → *"assignment"*

How to Compare Objects

This language also allows you to compare objects. To perform a comparison, you need to use any of these methods: "equal?", "eql?", "===", "=~", "==", or "<=>". You'll find all of these methods (except "<=>") in the class called "Object." However, most programmers override these methods through descendants in order to get proper semantics. For instance, the "Array" class of Ruby redefines the "==" operator. Because of this redefinition, two different arrays become equal if the number of their elements match.

The "=~" and "==" operators have negated variants, which are "!~" and "!=", respectively. The language interpreter searches for "!~" and "!=" first, invoking them if possible. If the said operators are not present, the interpreter will call either "=~" or "==" to negate the output.

The code given below invokes "==" to conduct the two comparisons:

```
class Example
  def ==(sample)
    puts "Let's compare self == #{sample}
    sample == "sample_value"
  end
end
example = Example.new
p(example == "sample_value")
p(example != "sample_value")
```

output:

```
  Let's compare self == sample_value
  true
  Let's compare self == sample_value
  false
```

The following table shows all of the comparison operators in Ruby:

The Operator	The Definition
equal?	If the argument and the receiver have identical object IDs, this operator will give you true.
=~	This operator allows you to compare regular expressions.
<=>	Programmers use this operator to perform general comparisons. It will give you 0, +1, or -1, based on the value of the receiver and the argument.
==	You should use this operator to check the equality of two different values.
===	People often use this operator in "case" statements. Basically, it compares the target with the listed items.
eql?	This operator will give you true if the argument and the receiver have equal values and belong to the same data type.
>, <, =>, <=	These operators allow you to perform basic comparisons.

The Case Expressions of Ruby

The case expression of Ruby is extremely powerful: it's a flexible "if" statement that has different kinds of enhancements. Since it has two different "flavors," Ruby programmers use this tool in most of their applications.

The first "flavor" is like a chain of "if" expressions. It allows you to specify one or more conditions and run a command based on the condition that will be satisfied first. Check the following code:

```
case

when game.name == "Ragnarok"

  puts "That's an old game."

when game.type == "RPG"

  puts "Cool."

when game.players > 1000

  puts "There are a lot of players."

else game.play

end
```

The second "flavor" is more popular than the first one. Here, you'll indicate one target in the top section of your statement. Then, your "when" clause need to have at least one comparison. Here's an example:

```
case command
when "debug"
  dump_debug_info
  dump_symbols
when /p\s+(\w+)/
  dump_variable($1)
when "quit", "exit"
  exit
else
  print "Illegal command: #{command}"
end
```

Just like an "if" statement, "case" gives a value whenever it runs. This value is equivalent to that of the most recent expression it performed.

The Loop Statements

The native looping constructs of Ruby are basic. Ruby's "while" loop runs its body until the result of the condition is no longer true. If the result is false at the start of the program, the "while" loop won't run any of its commands. On the other hand, a "while" loop might run forever if the condition won't evaluate to false. This kind of loop is called "infinite."

Ruby also offers a loop called "until." This loop runs its body while the condition is false. Thus, it will stop once your condition is met.

Similar to "if", you may use "until" and/or "while" as modifiers for your statements:

$x = 3$

$x +=1$ while $x < 50$

x # $\rightarrow$ 50

$x -= 1$ while $x = 50$

x # $\rightarrow$ 49

The Iterators

It's true that Ruby's looping constructs are too basic. This fact might have discouraged some inexperienced programmers out there. Well, you don't really need to worry. This programming language doesn't have complex loops because it doesn't need them. Ruby relies on its "iterators" to perform most of its loop-related tasks.

For instance, this language doesn't support "for" loops. Rather, it employs methods found inside different built-in classes. These methods are way much better than "for" loops in terms of effectiveness and reliability.

Let's analyze the codes given below:


```
5.times do
  print "Boom! "
end
```

output:

Boom! Boom! Boom! Boom! Boom!

As you can see, this format prevents off-by-one and fence-post mistakes. The code given above will run five times: that's it. Aside from "times", an integer may loop based on certain ranges by invoking "upto" and "downto". Additionally, each number may create loops using the "step" keyword. If you want a typical loop that goes from 11 to 20, you may write the following code:

11.upto(20) do |a|

 print a, " "

end

output:

11 12 13 14 15 16 17 18 19 20

To write a loop that goes from 2 to 10 by 2, enter this code:

2.step(10, 2) {|a| print a, " "}

output

2 4 6 8 10

In a similar manner, you may use the "each" method to iterate data containers (e.g. arrays). Here's an example:

```
[ 1, 1, 2, 3, 5 ].each {|val| print val, " " }
```
produces:
```
1 1 2 3 5
```

Chapter 10: How to Handle Exceptions

The examples you've seen so far were completely imaginary. Each call succeeded, incorrect information didn't exist, and system resources were infinite. In this chapter, everything will change. This material will introduce the actual world of Ruby programming.

Errors naturally occur while you are programming. Effective programmers and applications anticipate these errors and handle them with grace. In some cases, these tasks can be difficult. The codes that discover a problem might not know how to fix it. For instance, trying to access a non-existent file is okay in some situations. In some cases, however, such an attempt can be fatal.

The most popular way of handling errors involves return codes. You may use the method called "open" to return a specific value when a process fails. That value will travel through the different groups of invoking routines until something (or someone) takes care of it. The main drawback of this technique is that handling all of the error codes may be confusing and extremely difficult. If one of the functions invokes "open", "read", and "close" (all of which can encounter errors), how can that function identify the error codes it will send to the caller?

In most cases, you can take care of this problem using exceptions. An exception allows you collect data regarding an error and pass that data to an object. This object will automatically travel to the calling stack. It will stay there until the program finds the code that can handle the discovered exception.

Ruby's Exception Class

The object that holds the data regarding the exception belongs to "Exception", a built-in class of the Ruby language. The Ruby language has a neat structure for exceptions. As you read this chapter, you'll learn how Ruby's "exception structure" helps you in handling program errors.

In situations where you must raise exceptions, you may utilize one of Ruby's "Exception" classes. Alternatively, you may generate your own Exception class. If you'll choose the second option, you need to set your exceptions as subclass of the StandardError class (or any of its children); otherwise, the Ruby application won't catch the exceptions automatically.

Each "Exception" class has one stack backtrace and one message string attached to it. If you are defining new exceptions, you may insert additional information.

Exception Handling

The code given below utilizes the library called "open-uri". Thus, it can "grab" a webpage and save its contents into a file:

```
require 'open-uri'
web_page = open("http://pragprog.com/podcasts")
output = File.open("podcasts.html", "w")
while line = web_page.gets
  output.puts line
end
output.close
```

What do you think will happen if an error occurs during the process? Obviously, you don't like to save an incomplete webpage.

Let's incorporate some exception-handling statements and find out how they help. To accomplish this, you should create begin/end blocks and use them to hold the error-prone codes. Then, expand the blocks by adding some "rescue" clauses. These classes inform Ruby regarding the exceptions you need to handle. Since you placed "Exception" in the code's "rescue" section, you will handle exceptions in the "Exception" class and its subclasses. Inside your error-handling block, you'll report the problem, close and remove the resulting file, and raise the exception again.

```
require 'open-uri'
page = "podcasts"
file_name = "#{page}.html"
web_page = open("http://pragprog.com/#{page} ")
output = File.open(file_name, "w")
begin
  while line = web_page.gets
    output.puts line
  end
  output.close
rescue Exception
  STDERR.puts "Failed to download #{page}: #{$!}"
  output.close
  File.delete(file_name)
  raise
end
```

Whenever the program raises an exception, Ruby will place one or more references to the "Exception" object. That object will go to the "$!" variable. The example given above formatted the error message using "$!".

Once you have closed and removed the file, you should invoke "raise" without giving any parameter. This action raises the exception inside "$!". This technique is certainly useful, since it lets you write Ruby codes that screens exceptions, forwarding the ones you can't take care of to the upper levels. With this technique, you are setting up a hierarchical structure for error handling.

Your "begin" block may contain various "rescue" clauses. Each of these clauses may specify one or more exceptions to be caught.

The System Errors

Ruby programs raise a system error whenever an invocation to the OS (i.e. operating system) results to one or more error messages. If you are using a POSIX (i.e. Portable Operating System Interface) system, this kind of error might be called "EPERM" or EAGAIN.

The Ruby language collects system errors and places them in a certain exception object. Exception objects, which you need to define in the "Errno" module, are subclasses of the SystemCallError class. If you want to see the actual code of the system error, you just need to check the exception objects found in Errno. These objects contain the information you need.

Keeping Your Codes Clean

In some cases, you should run one or more processes before ending a code block. For instance, your program might open a certain file upon entering a block of code. Let's say you want your program to close the said file before exiting the block.

You can accomplish that using "ensure", a clause in Ruby scripts. Write each "ensure" clause after the final "rescue" statement. Basically, "ensure" clauses contain codes that always run whenever a block closes. Keep in mind that "ensure" will run 100% of the time, regardless of how the block closed (e.g. normal termination). Here's an example:

```
f = File.open ("testfile")
begin
  # .. process
rescue
  # .. handle error
ensure
  f.close
end
```

Most beginners place "File.open" within the block itself. This approach is incorrect, however, since "open" may also encounter errors. If that method raises an exception, running the statements within "ensure" isn't a good idea since there will be no open files.

How to Replay Code Blocks

There are times when you can solve the problems in your programs. In this kind of situation, you may run the "retry" command inside "rescue" to execute the "begin/end" block again. You need to be careful when using "retry" since it can result to "infinite loops" (i.e. loops that run forever). Analyze the following code:

```
@esmtp = true
begin
  # First try an extended login. If it fails because the
  # server doesn't support it, fall back to a normal login
  if @esmtp then
    @command.ehlo(helodom)
  else
    @command.helo(helodom)
  end
rescue
  if @esmtp then
    @esmtp = false
    retry
  else
    raise
  end
end
```

This code snippet used the EHLO statement to reach an SMTP (i.e. Simple Mail Transfer Protocol) server. However, not all Ruby commands support EHLO. If this process fails, the program will set "@estmp" (i.e. a Ruby variable) as false and repeat the attempt. If the process fails again, the problem will go to the invoker.

How to Raise an Exception

The techniques you've seen so far were purely defensive. The exceptions came from other sources. In this part of the book, you'll learn how to raise exceptions deliberately.

You may use "Kernel.raise" (a built-in Ruby method) to raise one or more exceptions within your codes. Analyze the example below:

raise

raise "This is a bad code"

raise InterfaceException, "Your keyboard doesn't work.", caller

The first line is the most basic. It simply raises a runtime error or the most recent exception (if applicable). Programmers use this syntax to stop an exception prior to forwarding it.

The next syntax generates a runtime error exception. Then, it assigns the string (i.e. the word/phrase/sentence between the parentheses) as the error message. Afterward, the exception will go to the stack.

The last syntax generates a new exception using the initial argument. Then, it assigns the string to the next argument. Lastly, the syntax will set the trace on your third argument. Usually, the initial argument is a class name or an object reference. Ruby typically produces stack traces through the method called "Kernel.caller".

Catching and Throwing Exceptions

The "rescue" and "raise" mechanisms of Ruby can help you stop your programs when problems occur. However, some situations require you to exit nested constructs while your program works perfectly. These situations call for the "catch/throw" mechanism of the Ruby language.

The example given below will help you understand how "catch/throw" works. This example scans words one by one. Then, it adds all of the words into a new array. Once done, the program will print the collected items backwards. However, you need to terminate the process if at least one of the lines doesn't have a legitimate word. Here's the code:

```
word_list = File.open("worllist")
catch (:done) do
  result = []
  while line = word_list.gets
    word = line.chomp
    throw :done unless word =~ /^\w+$/
    result << word
  end
  puts result.reverse
end
```

Here, the "catch" keyword creates a block using the name you entered (this name can be a string or a symbol). The block will run normally until the program encounters a "throw" statement.

Once a "throw" statement shows up, Ruby will go back to the program's call stack to find the appropriate "catch" block. If this process succeeds, the language will adjust the stack and end the block. Thus, in the current example, if properly formatted lines don't exist in your input, the "throw" statement will go to the last part of the matching "catch" statement. In this scenario, "throw" will end your "while" loop and ignore the codes that generate the required list. If you'll invoke the "throw" statement inside the second parameter, Ruby will return that data as the "catch" statement's value. Keep in mind that the second parameter is completely optional.

Chapter 11: The Basic I/O of Ruby

The Ruby language offers two groups of I/O (i.e. Input/Output) routines. You're probably familiar with the first group—it's the one you've been using in the previous examples. Check the following statements:

print "Please enter a number: "

name = gets

Ruby implements many I/O-related methods inside the module called "Kernel". These methods are: "puts", "test", "open", "gets", "putc", "readlines", "printf", "print", and "readline". With these methods, you can write Ruby applications quickly and easily.

The second approach, which offers more control and flexibility, involves the use of Input/Output objects.

I/O Objects – The Fundamentals

Ruby handles inputs and outputs using a base class called "IO". Because this class has two subclasses (i.e. BasicSocket and File), it offers different kinds of behavior. Objects that belong to the "IO" class serve as two-way channels between your Ruby application and one or more external sources. It's true that IO objects possess powerful features. However, as a Ruby programmer, you just need to write and use them in your codes.

How to Open and/or Close a File

Obviously, you need to execute "File.new" to generate new files. Here's an example:

The initial parameter serves as the file's name. The second one is called "mode string", a string that allows you to access a file for writing, reading, or both. In this example, you assigned "r" in order to set the file for reading purposes. Alternatively, you may assign "w" (i.e. for writing) or "r+" (i.e. for reading and writing). You also have the option to set the file permissions of a file you're creating.

Once you have opened the file, you may write on it or just read the information it contains. You need to close the file after using it. This way, you can make sure that all of the buffered information is saved and that the system's resources are made available to other Ruby-related stuff.

Well, Ruby can actually make your "programming life" easier: you may use the "File.open" method to open a file. If you will use "File.open" as a basic method, it's behavior will be identical to that of "File.new". On the other hand, if you will specify a code block in your call, the "File.open" method will show a different behavior. Rather than generating a "File" object, "File.open" will call the data block and pass the opened File object as the parameter. The file will close automatically as soon as the data block gets terminated. Analyze the following example:

This approach offers an additional advantage. In the first approach, the invocation to "file.close" might not occur if the program encounters an exception during the process. When the variable named "file" exits the scope of the program, Ruby's "garbage collection system" will terminate it eventually. However, system resources will get tied up since the removal process usually takes time.

The situation described above doesn't occur with the "File.open" method. If the program encounters an exception within the data block, Ruby will close the file before passing the exception to the invoker.

The Read/Write Capabilities of Ruby

The methods discussed above works for any file. That means "gets" takes one line from the standard input. Moreover, "file.gets" accesses a file object called "file" and take one line from it.

For instance, you may create an application named "copy.rb" using the following code:

```
while line = gets

    puts line
end
```

If you'll run this application without any argument, it will scan and copy lines to your system console. As you can see from this example, the program echoes every line whenever you hit

"Return" on your keyboard. Here's the code:

```
% ruby copy.rb
These are lines
These are lines
that I am typing
that I am typing
^D
```

The Iterators

Aside from utilizing typical loops to obtain information from I/O streams, you may use the different iterators offered by Ruby. The "IO#each_byte" iterator calls a code block using the 8-bit byte of an I/O object. The method called "chr" converts integers to their corresponding characters in the ASCII set:

```
File.open("testfile") do |file|
  file.each_byte {|ch| print "#{ch.chr}:#{ch} "  }
end
```
produces:
```
T:84 h:104 i:105 s:115   :32 i:105 s:115   :32 l:108 i:105 ...
T:84 h:104 i:105 s:115   :32 i:105 s:115   :32 l:108 i:105 ...
T:84 h:104 i:105 s:115   :32 i:105 s:115   :32 l:108 i:105 ...
A:65 n:110 d:100   :32 s:115 o:111   :32 o:111 n:110 .:46 ...
```

The "IO#each_line" iterator, on the other hand, invokes the data block using all of the lines within a file. The code given below uses the String#dump command to make newlines visible. This way, you will see that the technique really works:

```
File.open("testfile") do |file|
  file.each_line {|line| puts "Got #{line.dump}"  }
end
```
produces:
```
Got "This is line one\n"
Got "This is line two\n"
Got "This is line three\n"
Got "And so on. . .\n"
```

With "each_line", you may tag strings of any kind as line operators. It will just process the information and return line endings to the end of data rows. This is the reason why the output has several "\n" characters in it.

How to Write to a File

In the examples you've seen earlier, you called "print" and "puts", passed objects, and waited for Ruby to do what it needs to do. At this point, let's discuss what Ruby does in the background.

Using some exceptions, Ruby converts objects to strings by invoking their "to_s" method. Ruby will create a new string in case the object's "to_s" method can't provide valid strings. The code given below will illustrate this:

```
# Note the "w", which opens the file for writing
File.open("output.txt","w") do |file|
  file.puts "Hello"
  file.puts "1 + 2 = #{1+2}"
end
# Now read the file in and print its contents to STDOUT
puts File.read("output.txt")
produces:
Hello
1 + 2 = 3
```

The exceptions involved here are basic. Ruby prints "nil" as an empty string. When dealing with an array, Ruby will write the elements one by one as if you entered them separately.

You may need to record binary information and prevent Ruby from modifying it. You can achieve this by using "IO#print" and passing a string that contains the information you want to write.

Conclusion

I hope this book was able to help you learn the basics of Ruby programming in just one day.

The next step is to read more books related to the Ruby language. Then, continue writing your own Ruby programs. With this approach, you'll become a Ruby expert in no time.

I wish you the best of luck!

Robert Dwight

Made in the USA
San Bernardino, CA
05 August 2016